Listening to the Volcano

Conversations That Open Our Minds to New Possibilities

by David Hutchens

illustrated by Bobby Gombert

PEGASUS COMMUNICATIONS, INC.
Waltham

Library of Congress Cataloging-in-Publication Data
Hutchens, David, 1967–
    Listening to the volcano: conversations that open our minds to new possibilities / by David Hutchens; illustrated by Bobby Gombert.
        p. cm.
    ISBN 1-883823-62-5 (alk. paper)
    1. Communication in organizations. 2. Decision-making. 3. Organizational effectiveness. I. Gombert, Bobby. II. Title.
HD30.3.H88 2005
658.4'52--dc22
                                                    2005003232

Acquiring editor: Janice Molloy
Project editor: Kali Saposnick
Production: Nancy Daugherty

♻ Printed on recycled paper.
Printed in the United States of America.
First edition. First printing March 2005.

Pegasus Communications, Inc. is dedicated to providing resources that help people explore, understand, articulate, and address the challenges they face in managing the complexities of a changing world. Since 1989, Pegasus has worked to build a community of systems thinking and organizational development practitioners through newsletters, books, audio and video tapes, and its annual *Systems Thinking in Action®* Conference and other events.

For more information, contact us at:
Pegasus Communications, Inc.
One Moody Street
Waltham, MA 02453-5339
Phone: (800) 272-0945 / (781) 398-9700   Fax: (781) 894-7175
Email: customerservice@pegasuscom.com   info@pegasuscom.com

www.pegasuscom.com

5829   09 08   10 9 8 7 6 5 4 3 2

Chapter 1:
The Village of
Smoldering Pines

Once upon a time, there was a village called Smoldering Pines.

Smoldering Pines was surrounded on all sides by steep canyons and lay at the foot of the great, sleeping volcano, Mt. Discordia.

Its location didn't help the sluggish real estate market. But the views were nice.

This is Milo.

Notice one of the key differences between her world and your own.

Spoken words in Smoldering Pines take on a physical form.

Roughly the consistency of particle board, words can be carried about, used as trays to serve appetizers, or assembled into decorative planters.

Whenever people talk, their words appear in the air and then fall haphazardly to the ground. Homeowners then rake their discarded words into piles at the edge of their properties.

Over time, these piles have become fences. Whole neighborhoods have evolved, defined by *p's, q's,* and an occasional semicolon.

And so, in quite a literal way,
the very structure of this society is a product of
the things people say.

Oh. There's one more thing you should know.

Thoughts, like words, can become visible, too. A resident has only to twist her head firmly in a counter-clockwise motion until it opens with a loud pop and her thoughts come floating out.

Few villagers have ever witnessed this rare phenomenon, as their heads are screwed on rather tightly.

But when someone's head does pop open ... well, you'll find out what happens soon enough.

Besides these peculiarities, life in Smoldering Pines is rather similar to your own.

Granted, the town *does* lie dangerously close to a volcano.

But this isn't a concern for the residents.

After all, Mt. Discordia has been dormant for hundreds of years. What are the odds that it will suddenly awaken and threaten to rain fiery apocalypse all over the village?

Chapter 2:
In Which the Volcano Suddenly Awakens and Threatens to Rain Fiery Apocalypse All over the Village

One afternoon, Milo was in her yard scouting a place to put her new garden gnome.

Mr. Yaks, her next-door neighbor, called out to no one in particular, "Who left these question marks and ellipses on our side of the fence?"

"It wasn't me!" hollered Dewey Decibel from his front porch across the street, as he peered over his newspaper.

Libby Verbatim (who taught speech at Our Lady of Perpetual Enunciation) emerged from her home across the sidewalk and glanced at the mess in the Yaks's yard. "I believe those belong to Milo."

Milo was surprised. "Question marks? Ellipses? I didn't know … I couldn't possibly …"

"Ah ha! There you go again!" Mr. Yaks said, pointing to the growing pile of punctuation.

Just as Milo was about to respond, the ground trembled violently and a faint wisp of smoke appeared on the horizon.

"What on earth—," said Mrs. Yaks.

"Could that be …?" asked Milo, stunned.

"Agh! More ellipses!" Mr. Yaks called, tossing the periods back into Milo's yard.

The neighbors looked fearfully at Mt. Discordia.

A crowd began to form in the streets, as panicked villagers rushed from their homes toward the village square.

Milo, Decibel, Verbatim, and the Yaks joined them.

The crowded square buzzed with fear.

"The volcano is about to erupt!" a man yelled.

"When?" someone else shouted back.

"It could be days, weeks … who knows?" a woman responded.

"What shall we do?" another person wailed.

A voice called, "I've got an idea!" It was Mr. Yaks.
The crowd quieted. "When the volcano erupts, we
must climb the trees to escape the lava's reach!"
he declared.

Several others murmured in agreement.

In fact, the more they thought about this strategy,
the more reasonable it seemed. Within moments,
half the crowd was cheering: "Climb! Climb! Climb!"

As they chanted, their words fell to the ground.

"No! You're wrong!" hollered Decibel. "Climbing trees won't work. I say we stop the volcano! Let's ram a giant, fireproof cork in the top of it."[1]

The remaining half of the crowd saw a lot of wisdom in this position and began shouting: "Cork! Cork! Cork!"

As they chanted, their words fell to the ground.

---

[1] This idea was ahead of its time. It would be another three years before a fireproof volcano cork was available at Amazon.com.

The two groups faced off, shouting at each other with increasing conviction and volume. Verbatim joined the cork rammers while Mrs. Yaks stuck with her husband and the tree climbers.

Only Milo stood apart from the two groups. She watched as more words fell to the ground between the two sides.

A wall began to form.

This wall grew until the people could hardly see one another.

Frustrated, some even began throwing sticks and stones over the wall, which quickly escalated into name-hurling. (And in Smoldering Pines, names really *do* hurt—especially heavy compound words like *Knucklehead*.)

As discussions led to concussions, Milo found it curious how quickly everyone had taken sides.

The way we're using words is dividing us,
she thought.

It seems as though our words are good for making fences and putting things into groups.

But they're not getting us any answers, and they're not bringing us together.

They're not creating anything new.

The hour grew late, and the two factions slowly dispersed, each certain that their side had won the debate.

As the neighbors walked home, wading through a sea of discarded words, the Yaks continued to argue with Decibel and Verbatim.

Milo, deep in thought, was only vaguely aware of their discussion.

And then it happened: As Milo approached her house and turned to wave goodbye, she tripped on some stray exclamation points and fell into the flower bed, hitting her head on the garden gnome.

A loud pop sounded in the air.

Alarmed, Milo's neighbors rushed to help her … and then stopped in their tracks, dumbfounded.

"Hey, look at that!" cried Decibel. "I can see Milo's thoughts!"

"You're right!" Mr. Yaks said (agreeing with him for the first time that evening). "And it looks like she thinks we're a creative people!"

"No, no," Mrs. Yaks nudged her husband. "It says we're a *reactive* people!"

"Hey! I'm not reactive!" Decibel objected loudly.

Deeply embarrassed, Milo quickly stuffed the thought back into her head, closed the top, and struggled to her feet.

"I'm sorry, I ... I didn't mean to ...," she mumbled. "I really must be going."

Not giving the others a chance to respond, Milo rushed into her house and brewed herself a strong cup of Volcanic Soother herb tea.

It took her a long time to fall asleep.

Chapter 3:
Revealing Thoughts

Milo awoke the next morning to the lingering scent of burning sulfur. She glanced outside the window at Mt. Discordia.

Libby Verbatim stood in her own yard, doing the same.

Spotting Milo, Verbatim motioned for her to come outside.

"Good morning," said Milo.

Without taking her gaze from the horizon, Verbatim said simply, "I think you're right."

"I'm *right*? About what?"

"We are a reactive people. We respond to problems without thinking through all the possibilities, and we listen to the person with the loudest voice."

"Oh. That," Milo said, blushing.

"Seeing your thoughts last night was very … illuminating," said Verbatim, ignoring Milo's embarrassment. "What other ideas do you have hiding in your head?"

"I don't know. Nothing really."

Verbatim persisted, "Could you do that thing again?"

After a moment's hesitation, Milo glanced around quickly and took a deep breath. Then she gave the top of her head a counter-clockwise twist.

This time it opened easily with a gentle *whoosh*.

Milo and Libby sifted through the thoughts together.

Curiously, Milo didn't recall thinking some of them, at least not consciously.

And what was it about exposing these thoughts that made her feel so vulnerable?

Just then, they heard Mrs. Yaks's voice. "Honey!" she called to her husband. "She's at it again!"

The Yaks were soon outside beside Milo and Libby. They were quickly joined by Dewey Decibel, who had heard the commotion.

They all leaned in to stare at Milo's thoughts.

"How can you think we have other choices?" demanded Mr. Yaks. "We don't. We're stuck here in Smoldering Pines!"

Milo stayed calm and replied, "I guess I was thinking we don't *see* any other choices. So everyone keeps talking about the few that we do see."

"Then we need to start looking at other options that are less visible to us," said Verbatim.

"That's impossible!" exclaimed Mrs. Yaks. "How are we supposed to see what's invisible?"

"Maybe the answer is here," Verbatim commented, as she started to sort through Milo's thoughts, now scattered on the lawn.

For the next hour, everyone took turns looking at Milo's thoughts to see if they could discover the answer. Although Milo didn't enjoy the scrutiny, she tried her best to explain her thinking honestly.

Finally, Decibel declared, "Maybe there are more choices than I initially thought."

"I think you're on to something, Dewey," said Mr. Yaks. "Let's all get together again to talk some more."

To Milo's amazement, the neighbors all nodded.

"When?" asked Mrs. Yaks.

"Tonight at eight!" Verbatim said.

Meanwhile in the village square, the other residents continued their debate from the previous evening.

They felt confident they were making great progress, even though they were just repeating the same arguments with increasing volume.

An embankment of their words now divided the community right down its center.

During all of this, a smoky haze crept through the village.

Chapter 4:
Minds on Fire

As agreed, Decibel, Verbatim, and the Yaks joined Milo that evening. They were surprised to find that she had built a small fire in her yard.

"Come sit down," she beckoned them.

They each took a seat and stared deeply into the flames.

Milo spoke quietly. "Tonight it's your turn," she said. "I'd like for you to reveal what you're thinking."

There was an awkward silence as her neighbors glanced nervously at one another.

"I guess it's only fair," said Verbatim, and she reached for the top of her head.

Mr. Yaks reluctantly followed her lead, then his wife. Finally, Decibel did the same.[2]

Then they shared their initial torrent of thoughts.

[2] This exercise was especially hard for Dewey Decibel, who had to step inside, run his head under hot water, and then whack it repeatedly on the edge of the kitchen counter before it finally popped open.

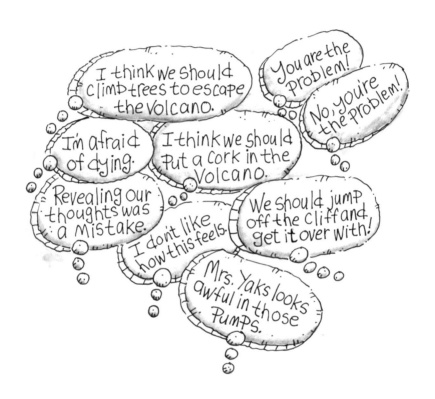

"I can't believe you think that!" Mr. Yaks exclaimed, pointing to one of his wife's thoughts about the crisis.

The group fell into an uncomfortable silence.

After a long moment, Milo prompted, "Try asking each other questions, like you did with me this morning."

So they did.

Initially, the neighbors were tempted to point out what they saw as right or wrong.

But by following Milo's lead and inquiring more deeply into what others were thinking, they became open to hearing new perspectives.

They began to recognize how what they said out loud did not always match what they thought inside, and tried to figure out ways to express their opinions more authentically.

Eventually, they could see possibilities they had not considered before.

Every night for the following few weeks, they met to talk in this manner.

Each time they conversed late into the night around the crackling fire, they felt a deepening trust and wisdom. The boundaries of their little circle seemed to grow larger and larger.

One evening after everyone had left for home, Milo sat alone, reflecting.

She was haunted by the thoughts Mrs. Yaks had revealed: *"What are we trying to accomplish? Do we really have time for this?"*

Milo shivered. It was true. They were spending a great deal of time talking.

When are we going to make a decision? she thought. *Or find some answers to our problem? That's the whole point of doing this, isn't it?*

Or is it?

That night, as the village slept, nobody noticed as a few flaming cinders dropped gently from the sky like snowflakes—the kind that have fire on them and can really hurt you.

Chapter 5:
The Eruption of
Mt. Discordia

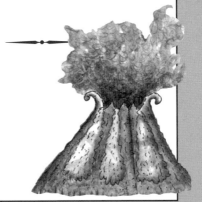

The next morning, Mt. Discordia erupted.

The earth heaved, and a thunderous explosion resounded in the air. Lava spewed forth in a glowing, orange stream down the side of the volcano and crept toward the village.

Terrified, the people flew into action. Some sealed their windows with plastic sheets and duct tape; others climbed trees. Still others ran around gathering bark to produce a huge cork.

Looking at the chaos from her window, Milo whispered to herself, "I guess it's all over."

She stepped outside. When she saw her neighbors waiting for her, she hardly felt surprised.

"We ... we didn't know what else to do. We think we should talk," said Mr. Yaks, bewildered. Mrs. Yaks and Libby Verbatim nodded. Even Dewey Decibel agreed without a growl.

It seemed crazy. Yet somehow it was clear to all of them that now, more than ever, they needed to continue their conversation.

As a fountain of fire filled the sky, the little group formed a circle.

With their heads open and their hearts racing, they talked about the crisis—and even their future. They shared thoughts. Ideas. Questions. Cautions. Impressions. Assumptions. Perceptions. Beliefs. Fears.

Throughout the conversation, their words fell to the ground.

Only this time, their words—combined with their thoughts—didn't fall into random piles, but somehow came together ... *purposefully.*

"Look! They have a bridge!" called out one panicked passerby.

Word spread quickly through the village. Soon, all the residents were hurrying over the canyon, carrying their most cherished possessions.

Safe on the other side, people clung to one another and watched in despair as the lava approached the edge of the village.

Milo, Verbatim, the Yaks, and Decibel, their faces covered in soot, looked on with mixed feelings of astonishment and grief.

Milo was deep in thought.

By changing the way we talk, we created something new that nobody expected.

We may lose our village, but I wonder ... what else can we create by changing the way we use our words?

Suddenly, the lava appeared to slow down. Everybody held their breath as the orange ooze engulfed one small hut and a cornfield, resulting in an explosion of popcorn.

Then the lava stopped.[3]

There were several moments of stunned silence.

Then the people began cheering wildly.

[3] The crowd groaned in disappointment when the lava halted just short of the Tax Collection office.

A villager approached Milo and her neighbors.

"Well done," he said. "Whose idea was the bridge?"

They looked at each other uncertainly. Whose idea was it?

"Actually, it was nobody's," said Milo.

"Or everybody's," added Verbatim.

The man looked confused. "An idea has to come from *some*body," he insisted. The people listening all murmured in agreement.

This made sense to Milo and her neighbors, too, and yet the idea truly did emerge from the middle of their circle.

"Can you teach us what you did?" a young woman asked.

Milo looked at her neighbors, and they all nodded. "My friends and I are getting together tonight," Milo said to her. "Come join us, and we'll show you how."

"Is it hard?" the young woman asked nervously.

"Perhaps," Milo replied. "Join us, and let's see what you think…"

The End

A Closer Look at

Listening to the Volcano

———•———

We live in a world of conversations. The ways we work, relate to one another, and create our desired futures are all shaped by the words we use.

On one level, how we communicate is obvious. After all, from our earliest days—even before we form the words "mama" and "dada"— we learn to connect with other human beings through speech. By the toddler years, children are keenly adept at getting what they want through the use of language (often more skillfully than their parents). On another level, so accustomed are we to using words to shape our reality that we rarely notice their influence. They're rendered nearly invisible by their omnipresence.

Maybe that's why we often find ourselves limited by our words. As often as they build, our words can divide, obscure understanding, and put a wedge between us and the people with whom we work and live. While we need words to accomplish our goals, they can also interfere with our ability to achieve what we most care about.

Today, many people in organizations are taking a fresh look at the ways we interact with one another. They're beginning to grasp important truths about our interactions: that *how* we communicate is at least as important (and often more important) than the content that we convey, and that by changing how we speak and listen, we can create shared meaning, new possibilities, and coordinated action.

Increasingly, people are employing the word *dialogue* to refer to this deeper form of communication—to the extent that it has almost achieved dreaded buzzword status. While the introduction of this word into organizational discourse has amplified our thinking about the most effective ways of communicating with each other, some misuse it as a synonym for "talk," as in "Let's dialogue about your memo for a few minutes."

But meaningful conversation is not a casual activity. It is a *discipline* at the heart of leadership and learning, rooted in ancient practice and ripe for rediscovery. By applying the tools of this discipline to the ways we communicate, we can surface and test our hidden assumptions, access the knowledge of others, create new options, and arrive at decisions that leverage an organization's best thinking. Further, by establishing meaningful conversation as a regular practice in our workplace, we can more effectively solve problems and make decisions, especially during times of crises.

Let's spend the next few minutes taking a closer look at Milo's experiences in the land of Smoldering Pines and see what insights we can draw about dialogue.

For Your Reflection:

1. By failing to consider the ways they used words, people in the story created barriers between themselves and failed to come up with creative solutions to their looming crisis. How does this resemble challenges you see in your own family, organization, or culture?

2. Think of a time when you felt changed by a conversation. That is, your awareness of yourself or the world around you was positively altered by your participation. What made this conversation unique? In addition to the content, what was significant about the process or the ways people contributed?

3. Why don't these kinds of conversations happen more often than they do?

4. Why do you think the subject of conversation is drawing so much attention in organizations? What is driving this interest now?

Creating Meaning Together

At its most basic level, there are two forms of human discourse. The first is one we are familiar with, because it makes up much of our daily interactions: *discussion*.

Theorists are quick to point out that the word *discussion* shares the same root—the suffix -*cussion*, which means "hit"—with words such as *percussion* and *concussion*. In that sense, discussion can be likened to a tennis match, in which words and meanings are hit back and forth. It is also similar to a closed container, in which meanings and positions are shuffled around within the boundaries until one person "wins"—either by having his point of view prevail over others' or by converting other individuals to his side. In some ways, our discussions are often just mutual monologues (like the debate in the village square of Smoldering Pines), with each person presenting her position in the presence of another who is doing the same.

Discussion is not necessarily conflictual. It can be a perfectly pleasant interaction in which decisions are made; tasks are accomplished; and order is established in your work, household, and relationships. But despite its usefulness, discussion rarely creates anything *new*. It simply shuffles and repositions an existing repertoire of options within the closed container.

The second orientation is *dialogue*. It comes from the Greek root *dialogos*, in which *dia* denotes "through" and *logos*, "meaning." Thus, dialogue can be defined as "meaning that flows through." Unlike the closed container of a discussion, dialogue is generative. It is an open and fluid process in which all parties are joined not as opponents but as participants who tap into a flowing stream of new meaning and emerging awareness.

Writers Glenna Gerard and Linda Ellinor contrast the differences between discussion and dialogue in this way:

Discussion/Debate	Dialogue
• Break the issues or problems into parts • See distinctions between parts • Justify and defend assumptions • Persuade, sell, tell • Gain agreement on one meaning	• See how the parts combine into a whole • See the connections between parts • Inquire into assumptions (our own and others') • Learn through inquiry and disclosure • Create new, shared meaning

Adapted from *Dialogue at Work: Skills for Leveraging Collective Understanding*, by Glenna Gerard and Linda Ellinor, © 2002 Pegasus Communications

As you may have sensed, dialogue is not a discipline that can be practiced casually. It requires an organizational culture that fosters trust, openness, and self-awareness—characteristics that are often alien to corporate environments. But for leaders who seek enduring innovation through authentic collaboration, this way of practicing conversation offers great potential.

The Distinctions of Dialogue

It's important to note that dialogue doesn't come in just one flavor. While different practitioners use different terminology, for the purposes of this fable, we will focus on two distinctions, what we will call "productive conversation" and "pure dialogue."

- *Productive conversation* is a strategic structure designed to create shared meaning around a specific topic for the ultimate purpose of making high-leverage decisions.

- *Pure dialogue* is an open-ended, divergent process centered on the discovery or exploration of meaning. It has no fixed topic and its goal is to generate new, shared insights.

Both forms of conversation require an environment of trust and openness; unlike pure dialogue, however, productive conversation is geared toward exploring a particular subject.

Many organizational practitioners who are engaging in dialogue are participating in the form we have named *productive conversation*. The reason that practicing pure dialogue can be so difficult is that it requires an investment of time—and no small amount of courage—to allow participants to release themselves to a flow of meaning that may at times feel frustratingly distant from pressing organizational issues. And yet, those who have deeply immersed themselves in the freeing process of pure dialogue over a period of time would argue that the payoff in terms of unleashing collective intelligence and promoting learning is worth the investment.

The challenge is to be purposeful in defining your desired outcomes. If you seek to build an organization of shared meaning and collective thinking—and you can summon the required patience and courage—there is rich reward to be found in pure dialogue. If the earth is shaking beneath your feet and you need closure around some new and specific possibilities for action, a strategic and focused productive conversation is probably the way to go. It's important to note that being able to have a productive conversation in a crucial moment largely depends on how well the organization has integrated dialogue into its everyday practices.

For Your Reflection:

1. Think about the debate that took place in the village square of Smoldering Pines. What are some disadvantages of this kind of communication? What are some advantages?

2. In your organization, what are some scenarios in which a discussion or debate is an appropriate form of communication? When would you use some form of dialogue?

3. Now think about the conversation Milo and her neighbors had around the fire in her yard. What are some pressures in your own organization that would make the practice of this kind of conversation difficult? Do the benefits justify the investment?

Mental Models

In the story, Milo made an important discovery: her words were connected to many hidden thoughts in her head—whether she was aware of them or not. The same is true in our world. This sensitivity to what is not readily apparent is an aspect of productive conversation and pure dialogue that separates them from common-variety discussion.

In the mid–1980s and early 1990s, physicist David Bohm wrote a series of papers in which he explored how thought is generated and sustained at the collective level. His inquiry into dialogue became the springboard for much of today's thinking on the topic. In *On Dialogue* (Rutledge Press, 1996) Bohm wrote, "Our thought is incoherent, and the resulting counter productiveness lies at the root of the world's problems." A cause of this incoherence, he said, is the belief so dominant in Western culture that thought is an individual phenomenon. That is, we consider thought a private activity that happens in the dark isolation of our own minds. *I think, therefore I am.*

But our thoughts don't exist in a vacuum. To illustrate, Bohm evoked the American Indians' open space dialogue and the ancient Greeks' practice of public discourse. These conversational structures encouraged a shift away from discussion and toward the emergence of a group mind that produces awareness and intelligence, transcending any individual's thought process. *We think, therefore I am, and we are.*

Participants must learn to "pop open their heads," so to speak—access the stuff that's hiding within—and share it with others who are doing the same. In other words, we must foster a collective awareness of our mental models. What are mental models? They are *the beliefs, assumptions, and images we hold about every aspect of ourselves, others, our organizations, and how the world works.*

A key insight of mental models is that they exercise enormous influence over us when they remain hidden. That is, we are frequently unaware of our conclusions, assumptions, and beliefs. We don't recognize them as mental models, but think they are simply the way things are. We assume the conclusions that are obvious to us must be obvious to everyone else. When others present opposing beliefs, or act in ways not consistent with our own mental models, the result is discomfort, defensiveness, division, stalemating, and incoherence.

To the extent that we become aware of our own mental models, we become open to the possibility that our own thinking is vulnerable to error or, at the very least, represents an incomplete view of the world. By recognizing and surfacing our assumptions and then presenting them to others in the process of dialogue, we create the possibility for new discovery about ourselves and our organizations and communities. As such, understanding our mental models is a shared activity in which participants take turns recognizing and revealing the hidden assumptions that inform what they say or do.

For Your Reflection:

1. In the story, when Milo first began to access her hidden thoughts, it made her feel uncomfortable. In what way does her reaction mirror your experience?

2. Now think about her neighbors' shocked reactions when Milo revealed her thoughts publicly. In your culture, organization, or

73

family, what are the social barriers to revealing thoughts and mental models?

3. In Smoldering Pines, people have a hard time opening their heads to access their hidden thoughts. Why do they encounter such difficulty? What are some conditions that would make it easier to identify and reveal your own hidden thoughts in a group setting?

4. What are some beliefs you hold that either enable or limit your effectiveness in your organization? In your relationships?

Advocacy and Inquiry

Now that we know how important surfacing our mental models is for fostering various forms of dialogue, how do we go about doing it? Let's explore two key methods of talking and listening, *advocacy* and *inquiry*.

- *Advocacy* is stating your views. It includes describing what you think, disclosing how you feel, expressing a judgment, urging a course of action, and giving an order.

- *Inquiry* is asking questions to get information from others. It includes asking others to explain their thinking step-by-step or for help in finding out what you may be missing.

Adapted from "Productive Conversations: Using Advocacy and Inquiry Effectively" by Action Design, © 1998 Pegasus Communications

Some principles for practicing advocacy include:

- Make your own reasoning explicit. Reveal your assumptions, state the conclusions you made, and explain how you came to those conclusions.

- Encourage others to explore your view. Invite them to test your assumptions. Reveal where you are least clear in your thinking and where you would like other input.

- Say things such as:
  — Here's what I think, and here's how I reached this conclusion.
  — This is my perspective, but I'd like to hear what you think about it.
  — What holes do you see in my reasoning? What am I missing?
  — What are some other ways we could think about this?

Some principles for practicing inquiry include:

- Ask others to describe how they arrived at their conclusions.

- State your reasons for inquiring.

- Avoid building your case when someone is speaking from a different point of view. Suspend judgment and try to understand why they believe what they are saying.

- Say things such as:
  — I'm interested in understanding your conclusion. How did you arrive at it?
  — What specific things did you see or hear that caused you to come to this conclusion?
  — When you say [X], what does that mean to you?
  — The reason I'm asking is _____.
  — You may be right. I'd like to understand your position better.
  — I'm really not understanding how what you are saying connects to what we are talking about. Could you say some more about it to help me see the linkage?

Adapted from the work of Refreshing Perspectives and their program, *Productive Conversation*.

By balancing advocacy and inquiry, we create the possibility for mutual learning and new insights. It can take a while, but the returns can be significant.

Poised for Learning

There's something else that must be said about the spirit of dialogue. *How you participate* and *who you are* in the space of the conversation are critical to the emergence of collective intelligence.

The ways in which you and your colleagues participate in conversation usually reflect the culture in your organization. Conversations wither in a culture that has been poisoned by mistrust, hidden agendas, and self-protection. Just as Milo did by creating a "reflective space" around the fire, organizations must constantly nurture an environment of safety and trust in which dialogue can occur.

In the absence of purposeful attention, we quickly fall back into a discussion mode that produces little learning. In my own conversations with my wife, my children, and my colleagues, I have observed with surprise how quickly and easily I slip out of a learning orientation. As others speak, I often have a belief that "I know where they're going with this point." I begin formulating my response even as they are speaking and often find myself impatiently waiting for them to finish saying what I already know they're going to say so that I can make my point. This is the default; it's the orientation we slip into in the absence of focusing our energy on learning.

But the product of this orientation is simple: We don't learn.

To shift this orientation, we must practice a skill labeled by some as *reflective openness*, in which each member participates with this mindset:

- This is only my current best thinking. I know there are other possibilities I do not currently see.

- My rank or position does not matter in this conversation. I am on equal footing as a human being with all of the others.

- I will silence my judgments while others speak.

- I can learn a lot from you.

- I expect to be changed by this conversation.

- I do not expect to persuade, compete, overcome, or win.

- I welcome moments of silence in the conversation.

Next Steps

Like all of the books in this series, *Listening to the Volcano* is not intended to equip you with the tools and skills to begin an immediate application of dialogue. Rather, the outcome of this story is to provide you with an awareness that can become the springboard for your continuing journey of learning. This is only an early step.

So where do you go from here?

- **Practice "reflective openness."** Begin seeking out people with whom you disagree and engage with them in a new way. Start with the orientation that "my thinking is vulnerable to error, and my beliefs are influencing my ability to engage effectively." Such is the orientation of the rare breed of human being known as "the lifelong learner."

- **Learn more about the tools and skills of conversation.** There is a rapidly growing body of thought and practice from which you can draw to deepen your understanding of this discipline. Recommended sources can be found on the next page in "Suggested Further Reading."

- **Create communities of learning.** Find people in your organization or in other areas of your life who may be intrigued by the offer of creating new possibilities by communicating in different ways. The reflection questions in this book may be a good starting point to help your group illuminate the need for new ways of talking and listening.

- **Solicit expertise.** Especially in your earliest forays into dialogue, you may greatly benefit from the expertise of an outside facilitator. By becoming involved with learning communities such as those at Pegasus Communications (the publisher of this volume) or the Society for Organizational Learning (www.solonline.org), you'll discover a growing network of thinkers and practitioners who can help facilitate your journey.

- **Pay attention.** Ultimately, all learning begins with you. Be purposeful in noticing how the ways you and others communicate contribute to your results. Become a student of your own thought processes, and develop a sensitivity to the activity that is going on in your own head when you speak, listen, and engage with others.

Are you willing to invest in the transforming discipline of dialogue? To begin, seek out others in your organization who are ready to take the journey. Find opportunities—both spontaneous and planned—to practice this new form of discourse.

Have courage. Practice humility. Unscrew the top of your head. Give it time. And the bridges will emerge.

Suggested Further Reading

Shadows of the Neanderthal: Illuminating the Beliefs That Limit Our Organizations by David Hutchens, illustrated by Bobby Gombert (Pegasus Communications, 1999)

Dialogue and the Art of Thinking Together: A Pioneering Approach to Communicating in Business and in Life by William Isaacs (Doubleday, 1999)

Dialogue: Rediscover the Transforming Power of Conversation by Linda Ellinor and Glenda Gerard (John Wiley & Sons, 1998)

Private Conversation: The Left-Hand Column by Action Design (Pegasus Communications, 1998)

Productive Conversations: Using Advocacy and Inquiry Effectively by Action Design (Pegasus Communications, 1998)

On Dialogue by David Bohm (Rutledge Press, 1996)

Republic by Plato (for some excellent examples of dialogue)

Turning to One Another: Simple Conversations to Restore Hope to the Future by Margaret J. Wheatley (Berrett-Kohler, 2002)

Acknowledgments

Whenever I first crack open a new book, I'm quickly drawn to the "Acknowledgments," never ceasing to be intrigued that an activity as seemingly solitary as writing a book requires such a crowd of people. (Perhaps even more so for this series: "Does it really take all those people to produce these silly stories?")

It does indeed, and in a living embodiment of the old "using a sledgehammer to swat a fly" metaphor, I received guidance and insight from the best thinkers and practitioners in the field:

The Reviewers:

LouAnn Daly; Ben Bruce, Spiral Systems, Inc.; Patti Russell, FedEx; Teresa Hogan, Refreshing Perspectives; Anna Doroshaw, Department of Veteran Affairs; MaryAnn Ahart, School Management Program, UCLA; Bob Putnam, Action Design; Glenna Gerard; Bill Isaacs, Dialogos

The Pegasus Staff:

Janice Molloy, Ginny Wiley, Nancy Daugherty, Rod Williams, and LeAnne Grillo

Special thanks to editor Kali Saposnick for her excellent leadership in breathing substance, warmth, and integrity into this "emerging" manuscript.

My daily partners in "meaning making":

My family—Robbie, Emory, and Ollie

If there is wisdom to be found in these pages, you have the above to thank. If there is foolishness (and there is certainly plenty of that), I alone am to blame.

Other Titles by Pegasus Communications

For a complete listing of Pegasus resources, visit
www.pegasuscom.com.

Learning Fables

Outlearning the Wolves: Surviving and Thriving in a Learning Organization

Shadows of the Neanderthal: Illuminating the Beliefs That Limit Our Organizations

The Lemming Dilemma: Living with Purpose, Leading with Vision

The Tip of the Iceberg: Managing the Hidden Forces That Can Make or Break Your Organization

Leverage Points For Change Videos

Leading in a Complex World

Teams That Work

Innovations in Management Series

Dialogue at Work: Skills for Leveraging Collective Understanding by Glenna Gerard and Linda Ellinor

PDF Articles

"The World Café: Living Knowledge Through Conversations That Matter" by Juanita Brown and David Isaacs

"Flexing a Different Conversational 'Muscle': The Practice of Dialogue" by Glenna Gerard and Linda Ellinor

"Dialogic Leadership" by William Isaacs

"Collective Leadership: A Process for Dialogue-Based Profound Change" by Kali Saposnick

Pocket Guides

A Guide to Practicing Dialogue

Ladder of Inference

Private Conversation: The Left-Hand Column

Productive Conversations: Using Advocacy and Inquiry Effectively

The World Café: An Innovative Approach to Dialogue

Newsletters

The Systems Thinker®

Leverage Points® for a New Workplace, New World